YOUR KNOWLEDGE HAS VALUE

- We will publish your bachelor's and master's thesis, essays and papers

- Your own eBook and book - sold worldwide in all relevant shops

- Earn money with each sale

Upload your text at www.GRIN.com
and publish for free

Bibliographic information published by the German National Library:

The German National Library lists this publication in the National Bibliography; detailed bibliographic data are available on the Internet at http://dnb.dnb.de .

Imprint:

Copyright © 2016 GRIN Verlag, Open Publishing GmbH
Print and binding: Books on Demand GmbH, Norderstedt Germany
ISBN: 9783668243446

This book at GRIN:

http://www.grin.com/en/e-book/334661/co-operation-in-humour-and-jokes-an-analysis-and-comparison-of-humour

Anonym

Co-operation in humour and jokes. An analysis and comparison of humour with reference to Salvatore Attardo and Andrew Goatly

GRIN Publishing

GRIN - Your knowledge has value

Since its foundation in 1998, GRIN has specialized in publishing academic texts by students, college teachers and other academics as e-book and printed book. The website www.grin.com is an ideal platform for presenting term papers, final papers, scientific essays, dissertations and specialist books.

Visit us on the internet:

http://www.grin.com/

http://www.facebook.com/grincom

http://www.twitter.com/grin_com

TU Braunschweig

Englisches Seminar

Introduction to Pragmatics

Term paper:

Co-operation in humour and jokes

*An analysis and comparison of humour
with reference to
Salvatore Attardo and Andrew Goatly*

Comedy is simply a funny way of being serious.

Sir Peter Ustinov

Content

Introduction

I will begin this term paper with an anecdote, my father told me. When my father spent a year in Scotland as a tutor at the University of Aberdeen, one of his friends invited him for tea at her parent's house. Her parents were a couple in their fifties and very conservative. They were aristocratic people, married for many years and never been abroad. My father was worried if they had prejudices against him because he was German. The atmosphere was very taut and mannered. The husband eyed him with narrow eyes, hidden beneath stern, bushy eyebrows. His wife sat in a chair, knitting. No words spoken. An extremely uncomfortable situation for my father. Suddenly their dog, a big wolfhound, started licking and cleaning the area between his legs. My father looked at the busy dog - thinking that the situation could not be any worse - and quietly said out of pure desperation: "I wish, I could do that, too." The husband responded drily: "I could hold the dog if you want to..."

This term paper will deal with the violation of maxims in the section of humour, mainly analysing the article "Violation of conversational maxims and cooperation: The case of jokes"[1] by Salvatore Attardo (1993) and Andrew Goatly's (2012) chapter "Pragmatics: co-operation and politeness" in "Meaning and Humor".

---

1   As found in Journal of Pragmatics 19 (1993), pp 537-558.

Paul Grice's cooperative principle

Before analysing the article "Violation of conversational maxims and cooperation: The case of jokes"[2] by Salvatore Attardo and Andrew Goatly's "Meaning and Humor", we have to focus on Paul Grice's cooperative principle (CP). Grice presented the CP in 1967 and his idea was that hearer (H) and speaker (S) have to speak cooperatively and accept each other to be able to understand each other. It describes how functional communication is achieved in a conversation. In Grice's opinion, society can only function communication if it is oriented towards co-operation[3]. He suggests that there is a way of speaking which we all accept as a kind of standard behaviour and that conversation and social interaction "is guided by the co-operative principle (CP)" (Goatly 2012, 225), which states "Make your contribution such as it is required, at the stage at which it occurs, by the accepted purpose or direction of the talk exchange in which you are engaged." (Grice 1975, 41-58). His hypothesis contains four maxims:

The Maxim of Quantity

- Make your contribution as informative as is required (for the current purposes of the exchange)
- Do not make your contribution more informative than is required.

The Maxim of Quality

- Try to make your contribution one that is true:
  o Do not say what you believe is false
  o Do not say that for which you lack adequate evidence

The Maxim of Relation
- Be relevant

The Maxim of Manner
- Be perspicuous:
  o Avoid obscurity of expression
  o Avoid ambiguity

---

2 As found in Journal of Pragmatics 19 (1993), pp 537-558.
3 If an utterance is uncooperative, Grice suggests that "through implication by the speaker and inference by the hearer, [it would] be interpreted as, in fact co-operative" (Goatly 2012, 225).

- Be brief (avoid unnecessary proxility)
- Be orderly (Grice 1975, 45)

When the S produces or the H hears an utterance, they assume that it will be true (maxim of quality), have the right amount of information (maxim of quantity), be relevant (maxim of relation, and will be understandable (maxim of manner). The standard implicature would be that if the S says the sentence:

"I have a cat." → 'I have one cat'

It is assumed, that the S has one cat, not two, ten or fifty, because in the case of quantity, the standard implicature would be, that the statement is made the most informative that could possibly be made (cf. Goatly 2012, 225-226). If we look at two examples, such as

(1)   A: "Do we have some tomatoes?"
        B: "No, but I will buy some at the supermarket in 10 minutes"

and

(2)   A: "Do we have some tomatoes?"
        B: "I'll go to the supermarket in 10 Minutes."

we can see that a particular intended meaning can be produced in a direct speech act (1) but also in an indirect speech act (2). If A was a competent English speaker, there would not be a problem, understanding that there are no tomatoes at the moment, but that B will buy them soon in the supermarket. Still both examples, direct speech act (1) and indirect speech act (2) deliver the information that there are no tomatoes. Thus we clearly have the flouting of a maxim in (2), we still do not interpret B's answer in (2) as nonsense, rather, we can assume that there is a meaningful message to be inferred. An implicature has been created and information has been delivered.

Salvatore Attardo's "Violation of conversational maxims and cooperation: The case of jokes"

In his article "Violation of conversational maxims and cooperation: The case of jokes"[4], Salvatore Attardo focusses on "how texts that violate the cooperative principle, such as jokes, manage to convey information" (Attardo 1993, 537). He presents the problem of the maxims as a paradox[5] because "all jokes involve the violation of (at least) one maxim of the CP" (Attardo 1993, 541), but still they contain and convey information. Attardo (1993, 541-542) gives an example (joke) of each:

Violation of the four maxims

(3)   Maxim of Quantity
        "Excuse me, do you know what time it is?"
        "Yes."

(4)   Maxim of Relation
        "How many surrealists does it take to screw in a light bulb?"
        "Fish!"

(5)   Maxim of Manner
        "Do you believe in clubs for young men?"
        "Only when kindness fails."

(6)   Maxim of Quality
        "Why did the Vice President fly to Panama?"
        "Because the fighting is over"

When looking at the examples above, we can clearly classify the violations of the different maxims. Example (3) does not provide enough information, so a violation of quantity has been committed. The question would usually be understood as an indirect speech act. The intention of the first speaker is, that the question will be answered with either a time providing utterance or a denial if the requested task can not be fulfilled. However the second speaker only provides the actual information if he literally knows what time it is. He fails to cooperate with the first speaker and violates the maxim of quantity by not providing all the information requested by the first speaker

---

4   As found in Journal of Pragmatics 19 (1993), pp 537-558.
5   See: "The paradox", p. 8.

(cf. Attardo 1993, 542).

Example (4) is a preposterous joke. Fish have nothing to do with changing lightbulbs, so the maxim of relevance is violated.

In example (5), the maxim of manner is violated. Puns for example are based on ambiguity, which should be avoided to fulfil the maxim of manner.

The last example (6) does not fulfil the maxim of quality. When Johnny Carson produced the joke in 1990, the Vice President has not been to Panama. He is presented as a coward, and with background knowledge, one would have known that the Vice President enrolled the National Guard to avoid being sent to Vietnam war, though there is no evidence that he would have avoided going to Panama (cf. Attardo 1993, 542).

The paradox

The examples (3-6) above show that each of the four maxims can be violated and still there are humorous results and a successful communicative exchange has happened. This result seems to be a paradox according to Grice's CP, because "on the one hand, joking is a successful interpersonal and/or communicative exchange, and on the other hand, joking violates the principle of cooperation, which accounts precisely for successful interpersonal communication" (Attardo 1993, 543-544). There are two options to get rid of that interesting paradox:

It can be argued that jokes are cooperative, because they 'work'; or that jokes do not truly violate the CP (cf. Attardo 1993, 544). If jokes show "the coherent organized pattern of intended meaning and received meaning" (Attardo 1993, 544), it can be assured that they follow a CP. It is not Grice's CP but some sort of CP. Attardo's opinion about Raskin's (cf. 1985, 110-114) discussion that jokes have a non-bona-fide (NFB) nature is very critical. He sees a weakness in it because Raskin pays too much attention to the role of contextual clues that contribute a transition from a normal communication-type to a humorous way of communication. In dead pan jokes for example those characteristics are suppressed on purpose (cf. Attardo 1993, 544-545). The most interesting issue, Attardo (1993, 553-554) mentions, is, what happens if the hearer (H) takes a joke seriously. If the H does not "read between the lines" and therefore does not "get" the metamessage for any reason, whether it is because of "personal feelings, familiarity with the joke, the teller, the situation, etc." (Attardo 1993, 554), a joke would have different effects on the H. If a handicapped person would make a joke about another handicapped person, it would be taken as self-humour, if the person was in perfect health and not handicapped, it could easily be taken as discrimination. At this point I

8

noticed that it is not necessarily essential to continue this discussion, because one year later, in "Linguistic Theories of Humor" (1994, 287-288), it seems that Attardo has a broader perspective on the CP cases:

> "It seems also that a radical dichotomy between "serious" BF [=bona-fide] use of language and "humorous" NBF [= non-bona-fide] cannot be maintained in reality. Grice's hypothesized speaker, totally committed to the truth and relevance of his/her utterances, is a useful abstraction, but should be considered only as such. In reality, speakers engaged in everyday communication use humorous remarks that hearers decode, interpret as such, and use along with other information to build their vision of the communicative context" (Attardo 1994, 287).

He adds that "[t]he consequences of this recognition – that communication which violates the maxims can still be "cooperative" - are far ranging." and that "[a]ny attempt to characterize linguistic interaction will have to incorporate rules and inferential mechanism to handle humorous violations of the CP" (Attardo 1994, 288). This is probably the problem-solving approach regarding the paradox that jokes violate the CP but still manage to convey information. The CP – in the case of jokes - is slightly different from the CP in the case of "normal" communication, utilizing Grice's CP. Andrew Goatly (2012) starts with another approach.

Goatly's "Pragmatics: co-operation and politeness"

Goatly (2012) deals with Paul Grice's co-operative principle (CP), Geoffrey Leech's politeness principle (PP) and Searle's speech act theory. He distinguished Grice's and Leech's principle-based pragmatics from Searle's rule-based pragmatics. Goatly agrees on Searle's theory that speaker (S) and hearer (H) have the agreement that locution (X), meeting condition (Y), stand for speech act (Z). He is convinced that the CP and PP by Grice and Leech are more guidelines rather than rules, which may be observed to varying degrees (cf. Goatly 2012, 224). He says that communication is structured in the way that:

hearer (H) → recognises the intention of speaker (S) and → utters the locution (X)

When it comes to breaking the maxims, Grice does not only consider the violation of a maxim, like Attardo (1993) does, he also introduces the

Violation of a maxim

If a maxim is violated, the hearer could be confronted with a statement such as

> (7) Two students (A+B) sit next to each other in a classroom during a physics exam. B
> has to rewrite a philosophy exam, he failed before. His teacher put him into a physics
> course so he will be supervised.
>
> A: Pssst! Can you tell me which answer you picked in exercise 12?
> B: Yeah, it's C.
> A: Are you sure?
> B: Definitely!
> A: Thanks!
>
> After the exam they meet in the hallway.
>
> A: Hey thanks for helping me with exercise 12. That physics exam was so
> freaking hard!
> B: So was the philosophy exam, I just repeated.

B knows that the other students are all writing a physics exam. When A asked him about exercise 12, he does not mention that he writes another exam, but gives him the answer to his exam's exercise 12. He knows that he definitely chose the right answer but does not share the knowledge, that he has a totally different exam than A. B violated the maxim of quality: he lied, even if unintentional, he did not share the knowledge, that he was the only one of the students, who was taking a different exam. In contrast to Attardo (1993), Grice introduces another way of breaking a maxim:

Flouting of a maxim

In contrast to violation, flouting a maxim is a noticeable way of breaking a maxim, which the S expects the H to detect. If the S uses the metaphor "Clark is such a chicken.", the S does not expect the H to actually believe him that Clark is a domesticated bird. In a flout, the breaking of the maxim is obvious and assumes that the CP is still in use which – through implicature – would mean that it still is co-operative. The following examples show that all maxims that can be violated, also can be flouted:

Flouting Quality

(8)   A: Do you like my new haircut?

B: Oh yeah, my mom used to have that haircut in the 70s.

(Irony)

(9)   "He knew that the child was his warrant. He said: If he is not the word of God God never spoke." (McCarthy 2007, 5)

(Metaphor)

(10) His mother is so fat that it gets dark 10 minutes before she comes home.

(Overstatement)

(11) Bob Marley wasn't an untalented musician.

(Understatement)

Flouting Quality

(12) Bubba: Anyway, like I was sayin', shrimp is the fruit of the sea. You can barbecue it, boil it, broil it, bake it, saute it. Dey's uh, shrimp-kabobs, shrimp creole, shrimp gumbo. Pan fried, deep fried, stir-fried. There's pineapple shrimp, lemon shrimp, coconut shrimp, pepper shrimp, shrimp soup, shrimp stew, shrimp salad, shrimp and potatoes, shrimp burger, shrimp sandwich. That- that's about it. (Movie: Forrest Gump)

Flouting Relation

(13) A: Dude that chick was so hot, I walked over to her and...

(A's girlfriend shows up)

B: Really? So James and Tom went to the cinema without telling you?

Flouting Manner

(14) A: I hear you went to the opera last night; how was the lead singer?

B: The singer produced a series of sounds corresponding closely to the score of an aria from 'Rigoletto'. (Levinson 1983[6])

There are three minor ways besides violating and flouting (infringing, opting out, suspending)[7] but I will not further exemplify them at this point, but continue with:

---

6   Via: http://www.glottopedia.org/index.php/Maxim_of_manner (10.12.2013).
7   (Goatly 2012, 232-233).

Goatly on CP and PP

Ever since Grice introduced his CP, humour theorists have shown that by breaking Grice's maxims, many kinds of jokes can be created. Goatly agrees to Attardo's (1994, 273ff) claim that "jokes and humour [are seen] as forms of non bonafide communication" but adds that "the breaking of the maxims must be recognised almost immediately, at least within the next couple of turns of the discourse for the joke to work" (Goatly 2012, 235). In contrast to Attardo's opinion in 1993, he later (1994) "points out [that] in terms of interpersonal relationships and entertainment, jokes are [...] co-operative, bringing about 'subversion of the maxims to achieve socially desirable effects'" (1994, 287). The thought that we need another way to classify jokes, than Grice's CP arises. Grice's maxims are principles by which we can make a conversation work, but now another linguist comes to the fore: Leech. Leech (2005) brought in the politeness-principle (PP) which defines politeness as a form of behaviour that allows us to communicate in a harmonious way. He uses different maxims which are tact, generosity, approbation, modesty, agreement and sympathy[8] which he later (cf. 2005, 12-17[9]) combined[10] with the grand strategy, which can be formulated thus:

"In order to be polite, S expresses or implies meanings which place a high value on what pertains to O (O = other person[s], [mainly the addressee]) or place a low value on what pertains to S (S= self, speaker)." (Goatly 2012, 239)

Leech also explains an interesting mechanism, called "banter". It deals with the phenomenon of joking between friends (15), which could be defined as a "ritual insult" (Goatly 2012, 243) that however expresses rapport.

(15) A: Don't you want to go to the barber before prom?
      B: Why?
      A: You look like Austin Powers.
      B: Yeah Baby! Yeah! Shagadelic!

Example (15) could have occurred in a different way, if B's hairstylist (C) was with them.

(16) A: Don't you want to go to the barber before prom?

---

8 Leech added "Obligation" and "Feeling-reticience".
9 In: (Goatly 2012, 239).
10 In: (Goatly 2012, Table 9.1, p. 238).

B: Why?

A: You look like Austin Powers.

C: Don't be so big-mouthed. I would like to see you cutting his hair.

As shown in (16), humour may fail for various reasons:

- the joke is not understood
- the joke is understood but not appreciated (Bell 2009)

To clarify the situation as joking, other strategies, such as laughter or smiling can be used to make sure that there is no face-threatening intended and that the communication is based on co-operative communication and not to be taken seriously. A joke could threaten the positive face of a hearer if the rules are not clarified. The relationship between S and H is important in this aspect. If a good – overweight – friend (H) enters the room and the S says: "Hide the pizza!", both would agree that, it was a mocking joke. There would also be the possibility, that (H) responds: "Then I'm going to eat you!", which would be a double rapport boost for both S and H. If the H was a stranger, he would probably feel insulted and the S would have hurt his feelings and threatens his positive-face.

Conclusion

Humour is a field of pragmatics which is not easy to figure out, because it is based on paradox, just like many jokes are. It can be said, that Grice's CP can only partly be used in coherence with jokes. Communication is based on at least two individuals, who are – as said before – individual, so a general rule cannot be used. S and H always act differently and while reading Attardo's and Goatly's texts, I noticed that when I read the examples of each violation of the maxims, I thought about people I know whose utterances, I would have interpreted entirely different, than the examples explained. For a general principle of communication, the CP works, but joking is a paradox itself, because there are many kinds of humour, such as black humour, bitter humour, irony, sarcasm etc. which would need a "rule" for every single facet. Additional, everyone knows people with no sense of humour, who (as H) would have threatened the positive-face of the S in every joke, told. The base has been created for the field of jokes, but in my opinion it is not completely figured out how humour really works in Attardo's (1993) and Goatly's (2012) texts. The closest approach was made by Goatly, who included Leech's PP into his theories, which takes away the rule-based character and contributes a kind of emotional concept.

Bibliography

Attardo, Salvatore (1993). "Violation of conversational maxims and cooperation: The case of jokes". In "Journal of Pragmatics 19, 1993. North-Holland. 537-557.

Attardo, Salvatore (1994). "Linguistic Theories of Humor". Berlin–New York: Mouton de Gruyter.

Goatly, Andrew (2012). "Pragmatics: co-operation and politeness". In "Meaning and Humour". Cambridge University Press. 224-246.

Grice, Paul (1975). "Logic and conversation". In Cole, P.; Morgan, J. *Syntax and semantics*. 3: Speech acts. New York: Academic Press. 41–58.

McCarthy, Cormac (2007). The Road. Vintage Books, a division of Random House Inc., NY.

Raskin, Victor (1985). "Semantic mechanisms of humor". Dordrecht: Reidel.

YOUR KNOWLEDGE HAS VALUE